"To help students launch careers

Sheppeck have provided students with a u

Industry: A Practical Career Guide for African-American Students."

"From concrete advice regarding attire, to psychological insights regarding attitudes, to illustrative examples, the authors have attempted to ma a chart to enable students to safely navigate industrial waters and establish an enduring and satisfying career. Hopefully, this book will be of value in helping greater numbers of aspiring minorities to penetrate what has been termed the 'glass ceiling' and achieve positions of power in the top ranks of industry."

"Certainly, for those students who have not had the exposure to role models or mentors, this book can be a reassuring guide to the world of industry."

M. Lucius Walker, Jr., Ph.D., P.E.
Dean, School of Engineering
Howard University

"...Easy to read in terms of the presentation and flow of information. The co-authors did an excellent job at identifying many of the problems young African-American professionals encounter, and offered very extensive and concrete advice on how to preempt and defuse potentially damaging situations."

"I recommend this book to all African-American professionals, both young and old. A book of this magnitude has been long awaited."

LaMar Prince
Financial Consultant
Key Brokerage Co., Inc.

"How I wish I'd had a reference like this when I graduated from college! It might have saved me the five years I lost just figuring out how to negotiate in a corporate environment! This book will be a lifesaver – and not only for recent college graduates, either."

Bettye J. Wilson
Director, Human Resources
IDS Financial Services, Inc.

"You have provided an outstanding road map for young African-American college graduates. The guidance in this book will enhance the professional development of all who avail themselves of your strategy."

Booker Rice, Jr.
Vice President
and Career Marketing Development Officer
The Prudential Insurance Company of America

"... enlightening reading for all African-American students. Lawrence and Sheppeck have produced a winner which is very informative, thought-provoking, and easy to understand. I found the book impressive in its content, and simply a superb career reference guide for all African-American students."

Gene Washington
Manager, Staffing and College Relations
3M Company

Continued on page 66

The Game Called Industry: A Practical Career Guide For African-American Students

Thomas Lawrence
Michael A. Sheppeck, Ph.D.

Black Collegiate Services, Inc.
1993

Library of Congress Catalog Card Number 93-73954
ISBN 09639245-0-8

Table of Contents

Dedication

This book is dedicated to the memory of Whitney M. Young, former executive director of the National Urban League. His tireless determination to bring about equality in the work place during the 1950's - 1970's paved the way for many of the positions African Americans hold today in American industry.

It is also dedicated to all African-American students who are striving to be the best they can be.

Finally, to our wives Caroline and Susan, we say thank you for your love, understanding, and support.

Foreword

Thomas Lawrence and Michael A. Sheppeck, Ph.D., have played the industry game and understand the inner dynamics of the corporate world. They also know the education game, which gave them a competitive edge in the writing of *The Game Called Industry: A Practical Career Guide for African-American Students*.

The authors make it clear that playing the "game" successfully requires a game plan that may call for a new vision of reality for minority students -- a casting out of the old models and perceptions and developing new ideas and paradigms to fit the new imperatives of the market place.

It's tough for anyone to compete within America's major corporations; however, it's generally accepted that minorities experience greater than normal barriers on their road to the executive suite. The tools needed to overcome those barriers are outlined in detail by Lawrence and Sheppeck. The traditional corporate values of loyalty, adaptability, advancement, and achievement are explored in detail with candid stories of real world examples of men and women who learned the rules of the game and played them successfully.

In publishing *The Game Called Industry: A Practical Career Guide for African-American Students*, Lawrence and Sheppeck have made a significant contribution to the literature on career-planning for African Americans. However, this book is an asset to anyone, regardless of race, who aspires to corporate success as this nation stands poised, on the eve of America's third century, to meet the challenges of global competition.

This is more than a sound and well-documented account of corporate access and progress. It is one of the best examples of "just in time" planning.

Companies that have received a "wake up" call about regaining the competitive edge are now aware that success in a global market requires drawing on the talents of a diverse population. As such, multi-culturalism will be the new corporate watchword of the 21st century.

This does not mean the glass ceiling will break easily. It simply means that opportunities for minorities will continue to increase and those who learn to play the game can expect to play larger roles at higher levels than ever before.

Thomas Lawrence is a frequent visitor to the Florida A&M University campus and has served for many years as a distinguished member of the University's Industry Cluster Program. He has helped to ease the paths of opportunity to corporate America for many minority students. Now he and co-author Michael A. Sheppeck have made it possible for the nation to benefit from their collective knowledge and experiences.

Frederick S. Humphries, President
Florida A&M University

Preface

It is cosmically inconsequential that I have known Mr. Lawrence for over a decade and that we have known powerful persons in American industry, but it is significant, and I believe that I can speak for many of my associates in education, that Mr. Lawrence, "Tommy", as we have grown to know him, has been a major influence in the careers of hundreds of African Americans during his industrial tenure with Honeywell.

In his travels throughout the country, Tommy has met and knows on a first name basis most of the African-American students in engineering and business. Truly amazing is his ability to nurture and assist these students unselfishly as they develop into professionals. I am delighted that he has taken this opportunity to record some of his thoughts and ideas so that even more students and educational professionals can benefit from his knowledge. In retrospect, I wish that such a success manual had been available for me many years ago. Students will appreciate the candid and factual approach used and can glean considerable insight into the industrial game.

For Tommy, thank you my friend. And on behalf of all students or former students, good luck and God speed in your new career.

Vascar G. Harris
Dean of Engineering
Tuskegee University

Acknowledgements

This book is our first attempt to assist African-American students as they begin to make career choices. We could not have accomplished this effort without the cooperation and guidance of many people. We would like to say "thank you" to the students of the following universities: Florida A&M University, Georgia Institute of Technology, Howard University, North Carolina A&T University, Prairie View A&M University, and Tuskegee University, for their participation in the survey which provided the data for this book. Thanks to Charles Johnson, Don Conley, and Foss Boyle, retired Honeywell executives who gave us valuable input regarding this project. To our professional human resources peers, who represent some of Americas finest companies, we say, "Thank you very much for your input and support." Dr. Fredrick Humphries, we thank you for taking the time to write the foreword for this book. Thank you, Dr. Edward Fort for your encouragement and support. To Drs. Harold Martin, Vascar Harris, John Foster, Ben Newhouse, Norman Johnson, Mr. Sam Hall and Mr. Leon Warren, deans and administrators of the previously mentioned institutions, we thank you for your support and cooperation.

Thanks to C.C. Campbell, Chris Bardwell, and Karon Rogers for your terrific editing job, and *THE BLACK COLLEGIAN* magazine for agreeing to publish and market the project. We give special thanks to Bettie E. Burditte for the many hours she spent transcribing this document. We would never have completed this task if it wasn't for her patience and understanding.

If we have overlooked anyone, we are extremely sorry, and we thank you for your support and prayers.

Tom Lawrence and Mick Sheppeck

African Americans in American Industry

The contributions of African Americans to American Industry is one of the world's closest held secrets. Names such as McCoy, Latimer, Woods, and Roebuck have received little recognition and, in the case of Sears & Roebuck, have been all but erased from public sight.

African-Americans joined American industry in large numbers only about 35-40 years ago. Even this would not have been true if it had not been for the historically African American colleges and universities that initiated technical and business-oriented programs following World War II. (World War II represents a milestone because a greater number of college programs led to more graduates who eventually would have an impact on industry.)

To be sure, a small number of African American entrepreneurs and business leaders existed from the late 1880s through WWII. Individuals such as Elijah McCoy (oiling devices), Lewis Latimer (electronics), and Arthur Gaston Sr. (insurance and construction), to name a few, were major contributors in their industries. These individuals, together with scientists and engineers such as Andrew Beard (the "Jenny Coupler" for trains), George Washington Carver (agriculture), Frederick Jones (refrigeration), and Percy Julian (chemical scientist), among others, contributed significantly to our way of life.

However, it wasn't until after WWII and into the 1960s and 1970s that African Americans began to play a major role in business. As mentioned above, the combination of increased educational opportunities and decreasing prejudice led to greater numbers of African Americans in professional and managerial positions in business. This growth has been such that the February

1993 issue of *Black Enterprise* magazine [1] could list 40 African Americans holding key executive positions in a range of American businesses. Nevertheless, even with this growth, African Americans still represent less than five percent of the technical workforce in this country. Therefore, the tenure of African Americans in industry, although a success story in the making, is still a painful but realistic history of what it takes to succeed in business.

It is now your turn to contribute to this legacy of African Americans in business. As each generation continues to contribute to the needs of industry, it will expand the opportunities for those African Americans who follow. Our hope is that this book will help you understand and apply the lessons the people mentioned above learned the hard way as you make your journey through the world of industry.

---

[1] Branch, S., "America's Most Powerful Black Executives," *Black Enterprise*, February, 1993, p. 78.

Chapter 1

Introduction: The Game Called Industry

Several books have been written regarding the role of African-Americans in American industry. However, we have found none which articulates how African Americans can achieve success and, ultimately, realize their highest potential.

Unlike the white male whose profile is often used as the standard, to hire African Americans, African Americans have little industrial history and almost no blueprint they can draw upon to help them reach unbiased success through the corridors of industry. There is no guide which helps them through this difficult maze, nor during the transition from college to the workforce.

As professionals, African Americans have been participating in American industry in large numbers just under 35 years, but they still haven't completely mastered "The Game Called Industry." One may argue, of course, that African Americans have been represented as professionals and managers in American industry for 50 years or even longer. However, for most of that time

African Americans held jobs as assemblers, matrons, or food service workers. Rest assured, we are not degrading these workers. Without this type of employment many African Americans would not have received the education and gains they possess today. Those jobs marked the beginning but, more important, they enabled African Americans to survive. But here we are speaking of the accountant, computer scientist, engineer, lawyer, financial analyst, human resource specialist, sales professional, and many other positions unavailable to African Americans in the early part of this century.

This book is meant to assist young people making the transition from school to their first professional job or those who have been in industry only a couple of years. The suggestions are based on the experiences and personal observations made by the authors over the past 25 years. Industry is a cold, calculated business. Companies are in business to make money and to show profit for their stockholders. One is naive to believe otherwise. Industry is a game that is extremely tough, and the game is not always played fairly. As one of the authors of this book (Tom Lawrence), I think if I had known how to play this game earlier in my career, I could have reached a higher level of my potential. My dad was a well-educated man with degrees in business, theology, and law. However, he was not allowed the opportunity to work in industry because of the vestiges of discrimination. As a neophyte in industry, I was at a disadvantage because Dad had no industry experience. I could not discuss my problems with him as my white counterparts did with their fathers. If he could have explained the "do's and don'ts" to me early on in my career, perhaps I would have been better prepared. Although I have had moderate success, perhaps if I could have tempered my ego and was more aware of my environment, I would have achieved more. Most African Americans do not understand that these are necessary ingredients to succeed in the business environment. I know people who have been very successful because they learned the game early. They understood the environment around them and, therefore, the game. Those who understand their environment, black or white, will survive and overcome whatever obstacles they face. I have an African-American friend who cracked the glass ceiling at the second tier of the company where he worked because he understood the company, its culture, and the environment in which he worked and played.

There are not many African-Americans who have reached his level. But, then, there aren't many white males who have reached this level, either. Yet, for anyone to reach this level, hard work and knowledge about the system are key factors.

Most African Americans who are about to enter into today's industry are ill-prepared to handle the day-to-day activities which are about to be thrust upon them. It requires time and often a painful learning process to understand the nuances that take place in business.

Granted, most have excelled academically, but they have not been prepared for a smooth transition from school to the workplace. The transition is a crucial phase in a young person's life. Initial exposure and experiences may very well determine the type of employee one may become, how long one will remain with a company and how well one will achieve personal goals. Many African Americans enter the workforce naive to the politics and behind-the-scenes maneuvering that take place within any industrial environment. Most enter their first job assignment with little or no knowledge of what is in store for them, and lacking true knowledge of the game, they are faced with the serious task of overcoming undefinable odds.

African Americans have overcome odds in other games, i.e., professional sports, but there the ugliness of racism was openly defined. African Americans learned to deal with it and went on to become superstars in their respective areas. They were able to excel in these activities because they understood the rules and the politics were out in the open. In the sports arena, they knew the parameters. They had a road map of previous experiences from dad, mother, brother/sister, and others before them. There was no similar legacy provided for many African Americans in industry as in sports. As students they received little, if any, counseling in four years of classroom work on how to operate in an industrial setting. Since most students have not received the "do's" and "don'ts" and the "how," "when" and, "why" at home or at school, they are disadvantaged as they enter the workforce and are on unequal footing when competing with their white peers.

To understand the industry game you must take time to learn about the environment before you enter it. Understanding the personality and the culture of the work environment is indispensable to success. You may have been a real academic achiever, but this is a new experience you may never master unless you take the time to understand your surroundings. If you are hired as an engineer, it is assumed that you can do engineering tasks. When you start that initial job, you are briefed about your assignment, the company benefits, its principles and its code of ethics. You also may be told that if you do a good job you will be rewarded. What you are not told about the politics, the unspoken behavior, and the emotionalism which, subjective as it may be, goes a long way in determining your destiny in a company. Understanding who the players are and knowing who is on the fast track (the one who grows within the company) are vital ingredients in making a smooth climb up the career ladder.

This book was written to help you make that smooth transition--to give you the information -- the do's and the don'ts, the how's, when's and why's that can make the difference between doing well and truly succeeding.

Chapter 2

The Transition From School To The Workplace

As a new employee reporting to work for the first time, you may experience some form of anxiety. It's normal; most new employees experience this. The intent of this chapter is to lessen these anxieties and to discuss the do's and don'ts of making the transition from school to the workplace. We will also focus on company culture, unspoken behavior, how to recognize who the players are, and what you should or shouldn't expect from the company.

We experience many transitions throughout our lives. Developmentally, we move from infancy through childhood and adolescence to young adulthood, middle age and, finally, old age. Scholastically, we move from grade school through junior and senior high to perhaps college, technical school, and graduate school. Economically, we may move from total dependence upon our parents to a level of financial independence. Of all the transitions we make, the one from education, whether from high school or college or graduate school, to the workforce is very difficult and has a long-lasting impact on our lives. But, even this transition has some identifiable characteristics which, if known in advance, may help make the transition easier.

When you first enter a company, two important match-ups occur. The first deals with your talents and the talent requirements of the job for which you have been hired. The second involves your needs and values and the needs and values required by the company. Exhibit 1 gives a visual representation of these "you-to-the-company" match-ups.

Obviously, if your abilities and other talents don't match the tasks to be performed on-the-job, you'll have a very difficult time attaining success in the company. We all have friends and relatives whose abilities and talents are minimal, but who succeed through tremendous amounts of motivation and simple hard work. While motivation and hard work will never go out of style, being prepared for a job through the development of the proper knowledge and abilities will make the transition to that first job significantly easier. Our experience is that those individuals who had a difficult time or failed at their first job were not suited for the job in the first place. They struggled or failed for reasons that were not as easily seen or understood by them or those trying to help them adjust to the workplace.

Each of us brings a unique pattern of expectations (i.e., needs and values) to a company. In order to be happy on a job and in a company, our most important needs and values must be met as we go about the daily task of doing a job in a specific environment. In other words, one way to define and understand satisfaction on your job is in terms of the fit between your most important needs and values and the potential of the job and company to meet those expectations. Job satisfaction results from the comparison between what you expect from the job/ company and what psychological rewards they actually deliver.

Exhibit 1.
A Match-up of You and the Company

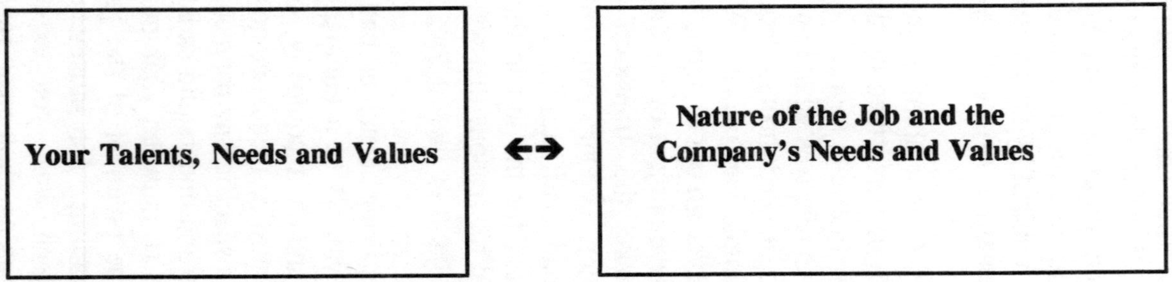

Your Talents, Needs and Values ↔ Nature of the Job and the Company's Needs and Values

On the other hand, your commitment to and identification with a company are also influenced by the match between your needs and values and the reinforcement received from the non-job climate of the company. This non-job climate is called the company's culture and deals with the fundamental values and assumptions deeply held in the company. Company culture gets expressed through various unspoken behaviors, internal politics, who gets to be a key player in the organization, how the fast track to the top is run, and a host of other sometimes visible and sometimes hidden symbols and behaviors. A mismatch between your needs and values and the company's culture may result in a strong desire on your part to leave the company at the first possible chance. More often than not, it's the mismatch between your needs and values and the company's culture that generally affects success on that first job rather than the lack of appropriate talent and ability.

Some Expected Do's and Don'ts

There are a number of simple do's and don'ts that may help you understand and deal with the fit of your needs and values to a company's culture. These are summarized in Exhibit 2.

Environment. It is important that, beginning with the first day of work, you become well acquainted with your new surroundings. Of course, this process should actually start when you are still on campus. Developing the right abilities for jobs in which you are interested; reading about the mission, products and customers of the companies to which you will apply; and asking questions (during the recruiting process) about the company and how it fits your needs and values will help you understand the company environment. Knowing where the parking lot, restrooms, and cafeteria are located is important, but knowing what is expected of you within your work environment is even more important.

You must quickly learn the environment's mores and the informal operating practices which make up the organization. You must adapt to the culture and standards of the company. You don't want to create conflict by acting contrary to the company's culture and expectations. Remember, in most cases, you cannot change the culture but must try to adapt as much as possible to it. Seeking out people who can help you understand the company will go a long way toward easing your transition from school to the work environment.

Time Management. Coming to work on time is a must and leaving late on occasion may be appropriate depending on your workload and priority projects. You must develop the attitude that your job is important, and you must be willing to give your best. Develop a habit of coming to work early and leaving late in order to get your tasks done; this will not go unnoticed by your supervisors.

Knowledge. Don't appear to know it all. Remember, you are the neophyte --the new person in the organization; therefore, you can't, nor are you expected to, have all of the answers. If you are confused regarding a task or you don't understand some procedure, don't be afraid to ask for clarification. Remember, there are people in the group who have knowledge of the job, and they are probably more than willing to share this knowledge with you. You merely have to ask. It's better to ask questions early or before you get into difficulty. Don't take on the attitude "I can solve this problem on my own." Remember, you're a member of a team, and good team members ask questions.

Socializing. It's okay to converse with a friend and co-worker, but this must be done within reason. Common sense should dictate the time you spend on what could be viewed as non-work related matters. Also remember that watching other people may not help you with this issue. Newer employees are generally given less "slack" on matters like being unproductive than are veteran employees.

Socializing on the phone is a "no-no." The phone on your desk is there for business purposes and it should be used primarily in that manner. Occasionally you may use the phone to take care of personal business, but the time spent on the phone should be limited to short calls. Incoming personal calls should also be limited to emergencies. Don't get in the habit of receiving personal calls on the job.

Participation in department activities is important. Get to know your peers and co-workers. Become a team player and be open to talk to as many people in the company as possible about their tasks.

Office Politics. Some degree of politics can be found in all organizations. This is true whether it is in school, government, or in church. Wherever there is a group of people, there is some degree of politicking going on. It is important that you learn the politics of the group. Early attention to this may save you grief later. You learn office politics by associating with a wide variety of people within the company and listening to what they have to say.

Interpersonal. It's important that when you first enter the company, you do not shut yourself off from the rest of the group. There will be members of the group whose personality you may not like, but as a member of the team, you must get along in order to get the job done. Don't participate in petty disagreements; if there is a disagreement, try to solve it -- not add to it! If you can't resolve problems, get your supervisors to help.

Mistakes. Humans make mistakes. Don't be afraid to make mistakes, as long as you learn from them and the same mistakes aren't repeated. Let others who might be affected by the mistake know that it has happened and that you're doing all you can to correct the problem. Then don't dwell on it! Learning should take place from mistakes. It's through mistakes, if corrected, that you grow and develop greater job skills.

Aggressiveness. Don't be overly aggressive. Be assertive - push for excellence at all times. Once you gain knowledge of your work environment, you will learn how aggressive you may or may not be. Remember, being aggressive in a positive manner is okay. Don't be aggressive to the extent that you become destructive either to yourself or to others.

Personal. Your personal life is not a topic for office discussion. Leave your personal life outside of the work environment. It is all right to seek advice from a close friend, but that is as far as it should go. If you've had an argument with your spouse, girlfriend or boyfriend, the workplace is not the place to talk about it. It's fine to share positive and good personal news with your co-workers, but remember, you didn't join the company to make friends -- you're there to do a job.

Education. It's crucial that you continue your education. It will make you more competitive and proficient in your career. Most companies offer in-house courses to keep you up-to-date, or you may opt to take courses externally. Remember that the company will not "come to you" regarding what you want from your job and the company. Therefore, in general, you should show that you are interested in continuing to learn and better your education.

We have tried to discuss with you some of the "do's and don'ts" expected of you when you enter the workplace. It's important that you adjust to your new environment as quickly as possible. Become a team player and learn as much as you possibly can about your assignment and the company culture. Perform to the best of your ability. Try to associate with those individuals who are on a fast track, because they can be of great assistance to you.

As we said in Chapter 1, African Americans tend to have fewer successful business role models. This makes it difficult to develop appropriate needs and values relative to organizational life. Understanding and adjusting to the culture of a company, i.e., the soft underbelly of organizational life, can mean the difference between success and failure for new employees. Therefore, you need to enhance both your job abilities and your understanding of what makes the company tick in order to be successful.

In Chapter 3 we present results from a small study in which recruiters from a number of large U.S. businesses identified the values their companies hold regarding work. These values identify areas in which African-American students need to gain more knowledge. We hope this information will help you achieve your true potential in "The Game Called Industry."

Exhibit 2. Do's and Don'ts of Dealing with a Company's Culture

Do...

1. prepare for the job by developing appropriate talents and abilities in school, internships, and through other work-related activities...
2. read about the company's mission, products, services and customers before going through the recruitment process...
3. think about your own critical needs and values relative to a job and company. Know clearly what you want and don't want...
4. ask questions about the company's culture during the recruitment process...
5. seek out a wide variety of people who can help you understand how the company really operates and what's important to its managers...
6. become acquainted with your new surroundings as quickly as possible once you are hired...
7. arrive at work on time and use your hours productively...
8. ask questions to learn the politics of the group..
9. take reasonable risks, but only when you have a clear objective in mind...
10. leave your personal life outside of the work environment...
11. take advantage of company-sponsored training activities and educational opportunities...
12. discuss any concerns you have with your supervisor...
13. praise others on your team and build bridges...
14. develop relationships - cultivate mentors...
15. work hard and make a commitment to the team.

Don't...

1. assume that the company will "come to you" after you are hired and try to discover what you really want from your job and the company...

2. shut yourself off from other members of the team...

3. be afraid to make a mistake and, if you make a mistake, admit it, learn from it and go on...

4. act overly aggressive in your work environment or you may run the risk of being viewed as too pushy or overbearing...

5. overdress or wear clothes which give the wrong impression -- you want your superiors to notice your good work. Remember, dressing appropriately is also part of the culture...

6. make a habit of coming to work late and leaving early--always recognize that someone is noticing you...

7. appear to know it all--ask relevant questions and pay attention to the answers. It is better to listen and learn. Absorbing the company culture takes time...

8. say anything privately or in confidence that is not defendable publicly or that you would not want to share with every member of your team.

Chapter 3

Work Values And Career Behaviors Companies Value Most

As we pointed out in Chapter 2, two important match-ups will occur when you enter a company for the first time. The first deals with your talents and the talent needs of the job. The second deals with your needs and values and the need-fulfilling capabilities of the organization. Your values or basic beliefs are your window to the world. In other words, they provide a foundation for how events are perceived and acted upon. Values help determine your expectations when you enter a new situation. Your reaction and commitment to an organization results in part from the match between your values and the reinforcement received from the job and organization. When expectations go unmet, you may act to change the situation, change your expectations, or simply leave the situation. Therefore, knowledge of your values and expectations helps others to make your transition as smooth as possible.

To gain a better understanding and perspective of the possible similarities and differences between an individual's values and the reinforcing capabilities of an organization, we developed two surveys. The first deals with an individual's work-related values. The second explores behaviors dealing with career development in an organization. The surveys are presented in the Appendix.

Both surveys were administered to a group of 88 African-American students at five major universities. They were also administered to recruiting experts from 22 Fortune 100 companies. The **work values** survey presented 40 statements that dealt with a diverse set of values relevant to the workplace. The recruiters rated the importance and expectations regarding the values applicable to their companies. In other words, they rated how important they felt the values were in their respective companies and how much an individual could expect each value to be present in their future work situation. The survey utilizes a five-point scale ranging from "do not expect this value to be present" to "expect this value will be present to a very large degree".

The second survey presents 25 behaviors that deal with long-term career success in one's chosen field. The recruiters rated whether they agreed or disagreed that each behavior was necessary for long-term career success in their respective companies. The students surveyed rated the extent to which they agreed or disagreed (on a five-point scale) that each behavior was necessary for success in their chosen career fields.

Work Values Survey

Exhibit 3 shows the 15 most important values (i.e., rated greater than 3.5 on the five-point scale) by the recruiters. The 15 values reflect three major value categories: performance, company policies and practices, and personal characteristics.

Performance

Six of the values show an emphasis on performing well within the company: achievement, ability utilization, job clarity, organization clarity, participation and productivity. Therefore, it's clear from the ratings of the recruiters that a strong emphasis on trying to succeed is something they look for in an applicant. In other words, their perception of you as a likely employee would depend, to a certain degree, on the extent to which you show the desire to achieve in various aspects of your life.

Company Policies & Practices

The second major value category deals with specific company policies and practices. The recruiters suggest that new employees should be concerned with advancement practices within the company; how pay decisions are made via employee comparison; and that the organization treat all employees with fairness and respect. Your interest in these areas will show that you are concerned about the type of company you work for and that you are willing to make an active attempt to understand how the company administers its personnel actions.

Personal Characteristics

The third major category deals with personal characteristics the recruiters feel are required for success. Specifically, these characteristics include a desire to make decisions about your work; the desire to be paid properly for your output; to continue your personal growth and development; and to work in an environment where you can maintain your integrity as you do the job. A strong personality orientated toward growth and integrity will ensure that you develop and grow from the opportunities given by the company.

Taken together, these three value categories, performance, company policies and practices, and a growth/honesty-oriented personality, spell success from the perspective of the recruiters. You should closely examine the importance you place on these values to determine if they match the recruiters' perspectives. Lack of a match suggests that you may find it difficult adjusting to a company's culture.

The Work Values Survey is presented in the Appendix. The 15 values rated as most important by the recruiters are in bold type. Take the time to go through the survey and rate the importance of each value to you at work. Then subtract the recruiters' rating from your own. Comparing your ratings to the recruiters', particularly for the 15 most important values, will help you better understand company culture and how to adjust to it.

Career Development Behaviors Survey

Exhibit 4 shows the results for the 12 career behaviors rated by the recruiters as most important for success. These behaviors fall in two clear groups: behaviors dealing with the company culture and behaviors dealing with the growth of your career. Items such as awareness of company politics; asking for new projects when things get slow; and working at your highest performance level provide a clear statement of the kinds of behaviors you're expected to show within the company's culture to ensure career success. In addition, the importance placed on behaviors like attending professional seminars; having a one- to three-year career plan; and identifying two jobs that you're shooting for in the next ten years show that many organizations expect you to maintain an awareness of your career goals and to consistently work toward them. These behaviors together with the value categories tell a story about company culture that you must internalize and adjust to if you want to be successful.

Students' Perspectives

One final note about the work values. Students rated four values as important that did not make the recruiters' top list. These values are: the ability to creatively uncover new ideas and effective ways to do things; the ability to achieve a positive or happy emotional state on-the-job; that the job provide for steady and secure employment; and the ability to have friendly interactions with others at work. These values represent areas where students may have expectations about working that are not shared by companies.

The student results were also broken-out by level in school: graduate students, seniors, and juniors. What we found is that younger students (i.e., the juniors) rated a number of values as more important than either the recruiters or graduate students. Specifically, juniors rated the values of honesty, fairness of treatment, and development higher than either of the other two groups. In addition, they also rated achievement and moral values as slightly higher than did the recruiters and graduate students. It's possible that younger students have ideas about what's important in business that don't exactly match reality. Their experiences haven't provided them with a clear picture of the daily activities within a business. The key point for you to remember is that industry prizes certain values and not others. If you learn what those values are and attempt to mesh them with your own view of the world in a way that is unique to your personality, you will have a greater chance of achieving success in industry.

So What Does It All Mean?

It appears from our study that students tend to put more importance on and have higher expectations for "soft" issues in organizations (e.g., creativity, happiness, friendly interactions, etc.) than do the recruiters. The recruiters, on the other hand, seemed to feel that a number of very practical and tangible values-such as performance and rewards-are important in their organizations.

When you enter a company for the first time, it's easy to hold very high expectations for the "softer," more intangible aspects of organizational life. After all, interactions with others and the chance to be happy, content, and creative are the things we constantly search for in all aspects of our lives. However, while very important to us, these values are likely to be less important from the company's standpoint for a new employee. Learning the job, showing a bent toward achievement, and being aware of and living according to the company culture are some of the values organizations expect you to emphasize early in your career. The more you live by these rules, the greater the chance you will "fit" into the culture.

Exhibit 3

Most Important Values Identified By Recruiters

	Value*	Recruiter Rating
•	Achievement	4.4**
•	Advancement	4.3
•	Ability Utilization	4.2
•	Clarity-Organization	4.0
•	Compensation-Compare	4.0
•	Compensation-Proper	4.0
•	Honesty	4.0
•	Fairness-Treatment	3.9
•	Clarity-Job	3.9
•	Autonomy	3.8
•	Productivity	3.8
•	Development	3.7
•	Moral Values	3.7
•	Fairness-Policies	3.6
•	Participation	3.5

* See Appendix for definitions of value statements.

** Rated on a five-point scale with 1 as low and 5 as high.

Exhibit 4
Most Important Career Behaviors
Identified By Recruiters

	Behavior*	Recruiter Rating
•	Awareness of company politics and who the players are	1.8**
•	Ask for new projects when things get slow	1.9
•	Work at highest performance level	2.0
•	Attend professional seminars	2.0
•	Admit when I have no expertise in an area	2.0
•	Identify a mentor	2.0
•	Have one-to-three-year career plan	2.2
•	Identify two jobs for the future	2.2
•	Change my work habits to suit the environment	2.3
•	Obtain a graduate degree in my field	2.3
•	Read technical journals in my field	2.3
•	Find out about career paths of those above me	2.4

* See Appendix for definitions of career behaviors

** Rated on a five-point scale with 1 as important for success and 5 as not important for success.

Chapter 4

How Companies Play The Game

This chapter will outline several practical approaches companies may use to deal with the value gap issue for young African-American professionals. The gap between your values and ideals and the reality of the company may easily lead to feelings of frustration and discontent. This is particularly true if you haven't had the benefit of past role models in industry. Organizations are beginning to pay more attention to dealing with these perceptual differences in order to hire and retain top African-American talent. We'll discuss some of the ways this is being accomplished.

A guide to this process has been presented by Richard Pascale in his *Fortune* article titled "Fitting New Employees into the Company Culture." [2] In this article, Mr. Pascale notes that "strong cultured" companies that are well-managed tend to engage in the following behaviors as they attempt to orient a new employee to the company:

• Put candidates through a very rigorous selection process.

---

[2] Pascale, R., "Fitting New Employees Into The Company Culture," *Fortune*. May 28, 1984, pp. 28-40.

• Subject the newly hired employee to experiences that make him/her question prior behavior and values.

• Have the new employee work in the trenches in one of the company's most important product or service areas.

• If the individual is a manager, measure his/her operating results and reward according to performance.

• Constantly stress that the new employee must adhere to the company's values.

• Constantly identify events in the company's history that reinforce the importance of the company's values.

• Ensure that the new individual has access to appropriate role models.

All these activities are designed to provide the new individual with a firm sense of the basic operating values and assumptions of the organization.

We have found that there are key criteria organizations often use to select and orient new college graduates. These include the student's GPA; identifying attributes of the prospective employee that fit the needs of the company; internship experiences; etc. We will discuss how these approaches are often made sensitive to the information needs presented by the recruiters' values and career objectives identified earlier in the book.

Grade Point Average

The grade point average (GPA) is used throughout industry as a screening device for specific employment opportunities. Although most recruiters indicate that the GPA is but one variable in the selection process, we have observed over the years that it is often used as one of the primary eliminators. There is a good chance you might be rejected if your GPA is omitted from your resume. This is clearly a blind rejection. What is acceptable? When recruiters are asked this question they most often respond that they are looking for a GPA of 3.0 or above. What about the student who happens to have a GPA of 2.8, is he or she worthy of consideration? Many students who fall in this category will leave their 2.8 GPA off their resumes in order, they believe, to have a better chance at being hired. In fact, by doing this, they have created suspicion in the mind of the recruiter. We cannot realistically and honestly explain the magical 3.0 standard. We can merely ask the question, will one do a better job with a GPA of 3.0 than a person with a GPA of 2.5? We suggest not. The problem with this index is that it is often over-interpreted by inexperienced and, on occasion, indifferent recruiters, thus eliminating individuals who could be successful in the organization.

The authors cite the case of Robert, a graduate of an HBCU. Robert, while carrying a full academic load, worked 40 hours per week to support a wife and family. He was rejected by several companies before being hired by his current employer where he has worked for seven years. One may assume Robert was rejected because his GPA was below the cut-off of 3.0. With a GPA of 2.5 from an HBCU, the pre-conceived notion is that graduates of these institutions are not as prepared as graduates from a majority institution. We suggest that you don't omit your GPA from your resume when applying for jobs. However, you must be ready to discuss how you came to have a particular GPA and what you are doing to adequately prepare yourself for a job.

Profile

In every organization there is a profile which suggests the type of people needed to make up the organization. This profile is typically developed from years of experience within the organization regarding the types of people who succeed and fail. Industry does a good job with the selection criteria when choosing a white male and also perhaps a white female, but most firms do a poor job when selecting African-American students to fit their environment. With the exception of a few, companies are recruiting and hiring African-American students who are wrongly placed in the environment. Both industry and the African American employee are paying a high price. Industry is faced with an endless turnover of African-American employees, thus providing poor return on their recruiting efforts. African Americans, because they are wrongly placed, never reach their potential. It should be evident that something is wrong with the selection process.

By "wrongly placed" we mean a mismatch between a person's talents and personality and the talent and personality needs of the company. For example, an individual with strong math and science skills might be placed in a "junior researcher" job that involves a great deal of working alone while preparing reports. However, if the individual is more socially oriented he/she may find the solitary work more a drudgery than an exciting challenge. He/she may feel the organization is deliberately trying to "break them in" by insisting that they perform this type of work. On the other hand, the career movement from junior researcher to researcher to senior researcher and finally research manager, may simply reflect the organization's accumulated wisdom about growth on this type of job. You must be prepared to ask a recruiter about the working conditions within the company and what is expected of the new person on the job. If the recruiter is a long-tenured member of the company, he/she may take the organization's culture as a given and neglect to discuss and explain the everyday routines that may appear illogical to a newcomer.

It is suggested that the profile used to recruit African Americans is that of a white male, which is unworkable in many cases. This profile typically emphasizes GPA (with particular focus on liberal arts courses), verbal skills, presentation skills, conservative dress and grooming, and a non-assertive personality. If we are correct, those companies which have not developed a profile to select African Americans which differs from the white male profile will never seriously close the value gap. Industry must stop looking for the super African-American student with a high GPA, who articulates well, is mildly aggressive, and well-groomed, to place him/her in an average environment; it just won't work. Many firms pay little attention to either the company's or your basic life values when making hiring decisions. Rather, they focus exclusively on your skills and don't try (or maybe even want to know) to discover what you are like as a person and how you might "fit into" the day-to-day operating routines of the company.

The key point for you to remember is that many companies are not sensitive to the unique set of talents and values you possess. They may attempt to gauge your potential success by standards more appropriate for individuals they are most familiar with: white males and females. African Americans have worked hard to achieve their capabilities and have such high expectations for success that inadvertently falling into a non-challenging job simply won't provide an adequate vehicle for showcasing those capabilities. Therefore, it's easy to understand why an individual under these circumstances might become frustrated and leave the company before ever having the chance to show what he or she can really do. Unfortunately, the majority of entry-level jobs are often non-challenging, which often leads to boredom and frustration. So you must be willing to personally manage this period of boredom and frustration with the ultimate goal of successfully adapting to the firm's culture. At the same time as you gain the respect of peers and supervisors, you may begin to exert your growing influence and shape the job situation to better match your talents and personality.

There are a number of strategies you may use to achieve this adaptation. First, set your sights on the long run. Growing into and becoming comfortable in a company takes time. It's like any new relationship, there will be periods of happiness mixed with periods of stress. So give yourself the time to fully understand how the company operates. Second, continuously talk with the long-tenured members of the firm about what it takes to succeed in the company. These individuals have adapted to the organization and grown with it. Find out how they approach their relationships with the company. Third, put as much time and attention into your job as it takes to ensure that you do outstanding work. Adapting to an organization is always easier if you are a valued member of the performance team. Finally, talk with your friends in other companies about how they are dealing with their adaptation. They might have insights you have over looked. You may achieve this shaping by describing your ideas about your job to your supervisor. Do your homework and develop a carefully thought-out plan for how you may improve your performance and better serve the company's goals by building tasks into your job that you enjoy. In other words, think about and describe activities for your job that both make you happy and help the company produce a better product or service. Take time with your supervisor to thoroughly explain your ideas and ask for his/her input about them. Then ask for his/her support in carrying-out the new activities. Therefore, you should be ready to describe your talents and values and show how they fit into the company's operating style. After you have developed your list of skills, life values, and work values, show them to the company recruiter and your new supervisor. Talk about what they mean to you and how you see yourself fitting into the company. Ask for their advice regarding how your talents and values may help or hinder your adaptation to the company. And by all means listen to their advice and plan to act on it to the best of your ability. Don't get angry over this lack of sensitivity, but watch for it and be ready to describe your unique attributes when a recruiter begins to use the wrong "profile" to measure your success.

Selection/Interviewing Process

This is the key process used by industry to determine if an individual is a good fit for the organization. The initial interview takes place on the campus during a 30-minute session. Following the campus interview, the next step in the selection process is the on-site interview. During this time you may find yourself on a whirlwind schedule of seeing many individuals during your visit. It may seem like everyone is asking you the same set of questions. It's easy to become quite stressed, tired, and bored.

The company interview usually has two objectives: to determine if you have the right talents for the job and for company staff to determine if you "fit" the culture. Therefore, the session becomes as much a marathon experience, testing your ability to remain calm under pressure, as it is an opportunity for you to showcase your talents. Be prepared for a grueling experience and work as hard as you can to maintain your composure and energy level throughout the on-site interviews.

Cooperative Education

This process allows you to gain real world experience while pursuing your education. It is one of the activities industry uses to close the employment gap between African Americans and their white peers.

While each school which offers co-op educational programs may have some unique features to its program, in general most programs are basically the same. A company works out the details of a program with a school which meets both the school's criteria and the needs of the company. If you have gained experience through cooperative education programs you may tend to do better in your job hunt. Theory is essential, but *real world practice* counts greatly. Recruiters and employers feel much the same way about hiring someone to do a job for them. They want to know that you have successfully done it before. If you have, then you can probably do it successfully again. This is why students who graduate with a co-op program tend to get better jobs. Their career-related work experiences make them better qualified candidates.

Internships

This process allows a company to establish work activities for students during the summer or during the school year after course hours are completed. If you have multiple internships with a company prior to graduation, the company will have an idea of whether or not it should make you a job offer. Internships give the organization the opportunity to observe you in action, like the co-op effort, in order to determine if you are the right fit for the organization.

Typically both co-op programs and internship programs are well-defined and well-planned. These programs are usually structured in such a way to give you a learning situation and the supervisor first-hand observation of your skill level. In addition to learning technical skills, you will also learn about the organization's everyday work values and required career behaviors. A knowledge of these "soft" areas is just as important to your future success in the organization as knowledge of the "hard" technical skills. An ill-prepared program can create a disaster for the company's recruiting effort. On the other hand, well-thought out and designed programs can be a plus for the organization's image and recruiting efforts on campus.

In summary, we have discussed various ways in which companies attempt to deal with the value gap issue for young African-American professionals. We discussed the importance of your GPA, the fact that a profile will be used to gauge your potential success, the selection/interview process (i.e., recruiting) and cooperative education programs. To achieve success, your personality (values, career behaviors, drives) must mesh with the culture of the organization. Working hard to keep your GPA as high as possible, understanding the profile of your unique attributes, and taking advantage of programs such as co-op and summer internships provide you with a better understanding of the challenges you will face on your first job. This also gives the company the opportunity to determine whether or not you fit its culture. We believe these steps are important ingredients which will help close the gap between African Americans and their white peers.

Chapter 5

Winning The Game Called Industry

Like Chapter 4, this chapter focuses on practical actions you can take to increase your awareness and understanding of the values and career behaviors identified as critical by the recruiters we surveyed. The focus will be on how you can achieve growth by understanding, shaping, and adapting to your professional environment.

We will be critical of what we believe is the "me" generation, so that we can show the trends that are causing many young African Americans to obtain false perceptions of how to win "The Game Called Industry." We hope that by citing some of the actions taken by young African Americans as they enter the world of industry, these actions will offer you a learning experience.

The Interview

In Chapter 4 we indicated that the interview is the process used by industry to determine if an individual is a good fit for the organization. You also should use this process to determine if the company and its culture fits your expectations and professional needs. Often young African Americans enter the interviewing process with little knowledge of the company. We suggest that certain activities must be completed in preparation for the interview.

Research

First, thoroughly research the company, its culture, products, assets, customer base, and anything else which will provide you with a good picture of the organization. Also look at the work values and career behaviors rated as important by the recruiters in the Appendix of this book. Develop some questions about these values and behaviors to ask the interviewer at the end of the interview. Find out how critical these issues are in the organization to which you are applying. These values and behaviors are a map to the real world of employment. Knowledge of the company will help you ask meaningful questions of the interviewer. It will also show the interviewer that you are truly interested in the company. Also, explore the company's community involvement to determine if it meets your expectations. Community involvement may be important to you from the standpoint of providing another mechanism to match your values to those of the company. Prior to the interview and during your research of the company, formulate questions you would like to ask; however, make sure your questions are relevant to the job and the organization.

Proper Attire

Another preparation is to leave your golf attire, earrings (male), and inappropriate hairstyles at home. Young fellows, it may be "cool" to wear a diamond stud in your ear lobe at a Greek Step Show, but it is a "no-no" within industry. Proper attire and grooming are a must -- dress professional. It is critical that you understand the importance of the initial interview. From this session a representative of the company decides if you proceed to the next stage of the selection process: the on-site visit. It is equally important that you understand that this criterion also applies to students seeking internships and co-op positions.

Internships/Co-Ops

We previously stated that the internship and co-op opportunities are processes which allow the company to get to know you and you to gain valuable work experiences and get to know the company. It is during this time that you can make a determination if the company is the proper environment for you. Again, using the work values and career behaviors in this book will help you to make this determination. You should ask the questions: **"How was my experience?" "Did I learn anything during my stay?" "Did I do meaningful work?"**

An important activity to help you answer these questions, as noted by William Granville, Jr., in his book *Just Say Yes*! [3] is to seek out a mentor who can guide you in these areas. A mentor is someone who will spend time with you and help you understand both the organization and yourself. Although it sounds as though finding a mentor might be a difficult task, there are plenty more senior and tenured individuals who are more than happy to give some advice to someone just starting a career. After looking around the company to find people who seem to know what's going on, simply approach one of them in the hall, cafeteria, or their office and ask for their help. Reach out to as many people as you can without becoming a nuisance.

You should come to a conclusion about the company meeting your needs after your initial assignment, and this

---

[3] Granville, W. Jr., *Just Say Yes*! Baltimore, Maryland: Career Communications Group Inc., 1989.

decision should determine if you will return, if given an employment offer. The internship/co-op assignment allows you to learn by practical experiences what you are studying in the classroom. They also provide you with insight into how a company conducts its business. One should have as many internships/co-op experiences as possible. The more practical experiences you have, the more your market value is increased. If you have had multiple internships/co-op experiences with the same company, we believe it makes good sense to start your career with that company if an offer of employment is made. Over the years we have witnessed young African Americans who have spent three or four summers with a company but rejected, upon graduation, an offer of regular employment. We believe this is a mistake. As indicated earlier, the internship gives you the opportunity to determine whether you are interested in working for the company. It doesn't take more than one summer to determine whether your personality fits the company's culture. Why not make a decision early on regarding your future? Most people experience temporary anxieties when they undertake something new. It is no different when you accept your first job assignment. Starting in an environment that you're familiar with helps to jump start your career -- you start with an advantage. If an offer of permanent employment is made, don't you think the company has an interest in you? Do you believe there is a loyalty factor associated with the internship experiences you have received? Do you believe that internships are something a company has to do or ought to do? Or is it a privilege for you to have such an opportunity? We believe that it is an opportunity when one lands a full-time job. An example should provide some insight into this. John X worked for company A for four summers in conjunction with a full four-year scholarship. He was offered full-time employment upon graduation by the company, but turned the company down because of its location. John X went to work for company B because it was in a more convenient location. Does company B have a concern regarding John's loyalty, even though they hired him? You bet they do! Although it may go uncommunicated, it may always be in the back of his supervisor's mind that John's **loyalty** is suspect. It would have been better for John to initially accept company A's offer for his own **personal and ethical** growth.

Loyalty

This value is an important one and will be important throughout your professional life. In the above case study, we discussed John's rejection of a full-time job from the company that gave him educational and summer intern opportunities.

We can understand the pressure placed upon John. He was the "right African American", the "right minority," the type that would "fit in." As human resource experts, we are critical of John and others who follow this pattern of paying little attention to personal ethics. Industry expects a return on its investment (ROI). No one does anything for nothing. Did John consider those coming behind him? We suggest not. It is important that you understand the moves or decisions you make. Internships and financial support are not provided by industry because they are nice corporate citizens (although this often is one of the motives). Previously, we mentioned that landing a job is an *opportunity*. Therefore, the company giving you the opportunity expects your loyalty. We define loyalty as a work value which mandates that you work for your organization as you would like employees to work for you. "Just enough" is not good enough! Loyalty is a value that requires your adherence to the organization's culture and philosophy. It requires teamwork, respect, and support of the organization's goals.

Adaptability

This value is very important when you initially begin your career. The process of learning your new environment and adjusting to the culture and mores of the organization is essential. The quicker you adapt, the faster your value to the team will be acknowledged. An organization's culture is built upon stated and unstated values and basic operating assumptions. The sooner you learn about these values and assumptions and decide how you wish to behave within them, the quicker you will assimilate into the organization and can show your talents.

Achievement

To achieve in any endeavor requires hard work. To achieve, you should set specific goals and objectives with distinct time frames for accomplishing them. Goals that motivate us tend to be moderately difficult, specifically stated, and totally accepted as something we want. Create your short- and long-term career achievement goals with these attributes in mind. The senior author once heard a speaker state, "If you always do what you always did ... you'll always get what you always got!" He interprets this remark to mean if you just do enough, it merely isn't good enough. In a dynamic organization, to truly achieve, you must go beyond the limit. This value does not come about through osmosis, it comes about through dedication and hard work.

Advancement

Within any organization there are only a few who will ascend to the top. If you want to be among the few, you must prepare yourself to accomplish this value. Complete knowledge of the organization is required. Understanding the politics and the key players is a must, but more important is an understanding of yourself. You must ask yourself what you are willing to give up or sacrifice to get what you want. The price you may have to pay may not be worth the time and energy you are willing to give.

Advancement is a goal we all say we want to achieve in a democratic structure. However, is industry a fair and democratic community? We suggest not. There are many barriers which prevent you from advancing, i.e. racism, company "fit," personality, and preparation, to name a few. Advancement takes many forms. Some people advance through an organization because they know someone. Others advance because they were at the right place at the right time. Some are advanced to the next position although they are not quite ready but are allowed to grow on the job. There is also a group who are predetermined to succeed and are sponsored and given the proper preparation to become entrenched in the "game." This group in some instances are the sons, daughters and family members of the owners of the company. They are being groomed to some day take over the company, i.e. Edsel Ford of Ford Motor Company. There is also another group -- graduates of the so-called prestigious schools, considered by American industry as the providers of graduates who have the talent to be leaders, e.g. Harvard University, Wharton School of Business, Massachusetts Institute of Technology, Stanford University, and Northwestern University to name a few. Many companies spend a great deal of time and money pursuing graduates of these schools; and, in many cases when they are hired by the company, they are on an accelerated pace of advancement.

Over the years, we have observed African Americans who have entered the workforce at a disadvantage because they do not understand how this type of game is played. In a hurry to achieve and advance, they become impatient and leave an organization only to find that the same circumstances exist elsewhere. Advancement is important in your work life. To take full advantage, you must have thorough knowledge of the environment and infra-structure of the personnel who run the organization. It is suggested that once you learn this process, you give it time to evolve for your benefit. To advance, one must be ***better than average***. Performing at the average level kills the careers of those who have the ability to be high achievers. The transition from school to the workplace is one of the most difficult you'll ever make. As William Granville Jr.[4] noted, it can be one of the unhappiest times of your life. However, you can take some steps to make the process go more smoothly. To do it correctly demands that you understand yourself (your values and aspirations) and the organization in which you work. Putting some time into the process of understanding organizational life today will pay huge dividends later, as you navigate your way through various jobs and companies. Be comfortable with people who drive themselves to excellence and try to emulate them. Find a mentor who has an interest in your career who is willing to assist you in achieving your goals. Remember, to gain the ultimate you must work toward it. We hope this book helps you set the correct compass bearing for your career in this "The Game Called Industry."

---

[4] Ibid.

Chapter 6

Real World Examples Of Industry Success Stories

In the introduction of this book, we suggested that to be successful in industry you must understand the environment, its politics, and certainly, the job.

This chapter deals with profiles of real people that one of the authors, Tom Lawrence, has known throughout his career. These people have reached a certain degree of success within their individual companies by employing certain work values which we believe are important in surviving the industry game. The names of the people and their companies are fictitious. However, as we profile their successes, we want you to know that their work values and work ethics are not make-believe, but are very real. By highlighting these work values and success stories, we hope some of their values toward work will be helpful to you. The following profiles may smooth your way to career success.

Ability Utilization

A work value which suggests that one does something that makes full use of his/her abilities.

Ralph Baker currently holds the position of director

of manufacturing for a large international pharmaceutical company. He joined the company upon graduating from college with a bachelor's degree in chemical engineering. He stayed abreast of the technology by taking courses and attending seminars relating to his field. He eventually received a master's degree in chemical engineering. Prior to joining his company on a full-time basis, he worked as an intern for three summers. He held several positions with the company from production coordinator, quality specialist, salesperson, design engineer, and process engineer to manufacturing engineer and several other positions -- either as an individual contributor or as a member of a team. These experiences, as varied as they appear, prepared him for the position he holds today.

For Ralph to have reached his current status, he had to have a willingness to undertake several assignments which he questioned at the time as being meaningful or even relevant to the position that he was initially hired for, **but he was willing to showcase his abilities and to do whatever it took to get the job done**. He performed each assignment well because he knew he was adding to his portfolio. Ralph's profile depicts a person who used his abilities to gain success. He understood the parameters of his environment, he knew and understood the decision-making process and, most importantly, what was required of him to move up the company's ladder. We all have unique values and abilities. We suggest that you take an inventory of your work-related values and abilities. Determine what you need to do to gain maximum use of your talents: this will allow you to progress in the organization. We believe Ralph did this. You may ask why Ralph wanted to stay abreast of the technology? We believe he wanted to stay abreast because he observed that the people around him who were advancing were the people who took courses to improve themselves and better prepare themselves for their next assignment. Ralph understood that it was a must to have as many different types of assignments and use as many of his abilities as possible if he was to be considered for future promotions. He modeled his career after others who came before him. Normally, people who reach a certain level are people who are multi-dimensional in their abilities and are therefore prepared to handle any situation.

We believe that having many assignments gives you an opportunity to use all your talents rather than focusing on just a few. It also builds perspective about the way the company operates. Once you determine what you need to do to gain maximum use of your talents, then set your course. Once your course is set and you are prepared, progress will take place as it did in Ralph's case.

Advancement

A work value which provides an advancement opportunity in the organization when one is willing to work hard and adapt to various situations which may deviate from one's normal routine of activities.

Reed Smith is a vice president and general manager of a diversified international high-technology company. Reed started his career a year after graduating from college with an MBA in marketing, when he joined the company that offered him the most money. When he found that the environment would not allow him to use his talents and provided no real avenues for advancement, he became frustrated and decided to leave. Although Reed initially turned his present company down, he had impressed the staffing representatives during a prior interview. When they learned that Reed was looking for other opportunities, they convinced the company to offer Reed an opportunity. He started as a personnel representative for the solid state electronics division. Within five years, he became the personnel manager. Two years later, he became personnel director of the component business, which was made up of several divisions. His next assignment was director of marketing for the coils division. He remained in this position for three years, until he was promoted to vice president and general manager of the solid state electronics division, his current position. Reed had to relocate several times during his career, which created some hardships and adjustments for his family, but they were willing to endure them to enhance his career. Reed and Tommy have talked on several occasions regarding his successful career. During each discussion it was evident that he *had a career plan and a goal of attainment he'd set for himself* when he joined the company. We are often faced with obstacles and sometimes as individuals, we become sidetracked and never reach our potential. On the other hand, there are people we admire because they appear to have the determination to do whatever it takes to achieve. It was apparent that Reed was on a journey and he wasn't merely seeking a destination. Through his tenacity and determination, Reed designed an ambitious plan to achieve success.

It is obvious that Reed was willing to take on several different types of assignments and uproot his family, exposing them to different cities and, in many cases, different environments in order to advance. *Adaptation* and *adjustment* are key ingredients in Reed's profile. Reed discussed his career with several people that he respected and admired. He realized that by taking on different assignments that they became critical components for success. During Reed's journey he made and corrected mistakes, which made him a better employee. With the support of his family he pursued his quest to achieve success. Reed accomplished his goal.

Achievement-Competition

A combination of work values: Achievement illustrates that the job gives one a feeling of personal accomplishment. Competition allows one to compete against others based upon a clear standard of excellence.

Willis Garth graduated with a bachelor's degree in marketing and went to work for a major retail company. He is currently senior vice president of merchandise. Willis started his career as a stock coordinator. However, when he discusses his initial position, he says he was a glorified stockboy. But he is also quick to say that this is how he learned the retail business. Willis says his personality, arrogance, aggressiveness, and the desire to learn, adapt, and work hard propelled him to the top position he has held for the past eight years. His *willingness to take chances* and his knowledge of the business have earned him a great deal of respect in the retail business.

I once heard Willis give a speech where he challenged his college audience to be risk-takers and to enter businesses whose environment would afford them the opportunities to take risks. The company has allowed Willis to take risks and compete, and with his self-confidence adapted to fit the company culture, he has enhanced his own self-worth and achieved a high degree of excellence while participating in a very competitive industry. It is evident that through his competitive spirit and the desire to achieve, Willis applied those values that allowed him to become successful. If you have a good image of yourself which suggests that you can achieve whatever you undertake, then you have established a vision of strength. Willis, with a good self image and a competitive drive, was able to translate his arrogance and aggressiveness into positive competition and ultimate achievement. If you are committed to compete for excellence, then you will find success. Willis showed this commitment and was rewarded. This story shows the importance of going into an industry where there is synergy between your personality and the nature of the business. If achievement is working hard to attain a sense of personal accomplishment, Willis' story shows that it is important that you select a company which will accept your personality. In other words, feeling the need to accomplish and being an aggressive competitor can lead to negative interactions with others in a non-receptive environment and ultimately destroy your career. If the environment is right for your personality we suggest that you show that competitive attitude and strive to make a difference.

Hard Work

This work value suggests that to achieve, one must give all his or her energy to achieve success. Success will not be recognized if one doesn't do his/her best.

Nancy Blue graduated from college with a bachelor's degree in political science. After graduating, she went to work for a major computer manufacturing company as a personnel assistant in its human resources department. She was conscientious and excelled in each assignment she was given. Recognizing that her ultimate goal was to attend law school, Nancy held several human resource management jobs while pursuing her law degree. She is currently the chief patent attorney for the company. Nancy obtained this status by understanding her environment, what was expected of her, applying proper work ethics to her assignment, **working hard,** and by developing a plan to achieve her self-declared goal. It was obvious that Nancy was committed to achieve. Through hard work, pride, integrity, and a determination to excel, Nancy navigated herself to success. She gained her current position because she was committed to quality and excellence which are valuable commodities for obtaining success. It was obvious that Nancy had a goal to reach. Working a full-time job while attending law school she was often faced with a 60-70 hour week early in her career. She didn't have much of a social life, which she admits was sometimes lonely and frustrating; however, she was willing to put this aspect of her life on hold.

Nancy was able to accomplish her goal because of her self dedication and the support of a mentor she selected, who was interested in her career and supported her with knowledge, kindness, and understanding. Nancy's story shows that the work value of working hard means balancing multiple competing priorities at the same time. The lesson here is that you should be willing to set goals, prioritize them and work hard to achieve them. Throughout this chapter we have tried to share with you profiles of people who have made it in industry. There is a common theme associated with each person profiled and ***that is a desire to achieve, a desire to utilize his or her abilities, a desire to compete and to work hard.*** It is also obvious that if you establish realistic goals and if you work hard and do what is necessary to attain those goals, you will be successful.

Conclusion

Our experience working and helping others in business over the past 25 years tells us that the strategies contained in this book will help you make a smooth transition from school to the work place. As we stated in Chapter 2, understanding and adjusting to the culture of an organization is just as important to personal success as having the right skills for the job. So you need to fully understand both yourself (your needs, values, skills and aspirations) and the nature of the organization in which you will be working. A lack of this understanding is a prescription for failure. Don't let it happen to you!

We hope that students, new professionals, and corporate managers will consult this book regularly. Doing so will serve as a constant reminder of the importance of mutual understanding; i.e., both the organization and its employees comprehending what each needs to be productive and fulfilled today and into the future. Our sincere hope is that all the readers of this book will achieve greater success for themselves and their organizations by using this important roadmap for mutual knowledge and respect.

Appendix

Completing the Work Value and Career Behavior Surveys for Yourself

This Appendix contains blank copies of the Work Value and Career Behavior Surveys used as a part of this book. You may complete the surveys and compare your responses to those of the company recruiters. Remember, it's critical that you be as truthful as possible if these surveys are to help you determine what drives you in a job, organization, and career.

Work Values Profile

The Work Values Profile lists 41 values that relate to working life. Each value is rated both in terms of importance to you at work and in terms of the extent to which you expect the value to be present in your future work situation. Follow the instructions at the front of the survey to complete your ratings.

Survey Interpretation

The summary ratings from the 22 recruiters (identified earlier in the book) are presented on the right side of the survey. After you have completed your ratings, compare them with those of the recruiters. For each value statement, subtract the recruiters' ratings from your own and place the difference on the blank on the right side of the page.

Review all the bold print value statements (rated 4 or 5 by the recruiters). Check to see if the difference between your rating and theirs on those items are either zero or a positive number. (A difference of zero or a positive number indicates that you also view the item as very important.) If the difference between your rating and the recruiters' on those items is a negative number, it means that you are not aware of the importance of those values in the work setting. This represents a situation where you expect to find one thing when you start your career, but actually find something very different.

Finally, review all the value statements rated either a 1 or 2 by the recruiters. Check to see if the difference between your ratings and theirs on those items are either zero or a negative number. (A difference of zero or a negative number indicates that you also view the item as either not very important.) If the difference between your rating and the recruiters' on those items is a positive number, it means that you expect to find this value in your future work situation, when in fact it may not exist.

Career Behaviors Profile

The Career Behaviors Profile lists 25 behaviors that are necessary for long-term career success in your chosen field. Each behavior is rated according to how much you agree or disagree that the behavior is necessary for career success. Follow the instructions at the front of the survey to complete your ratings of the career behaviors.

Survey Interpretation

Like the Work Values Profile, the right side of the page shows the summary ratings from 22 recruiters identified earlier in the book. After you have completed your ratings, compare your ratings with the recruiters' results. For each behavior, subtract the recruiters' rating from your own and place the difference on the blank at the right of the page.

Review all the behaviors rated as either a 1 or 2 by the recruiters (i.e., necessary for career success). Check to see if the difference between your ratings and theirs on those items is either zero or a negative number. (A difference of zero or a negative number would indicate that you also agree that the item is necessary for career success.) If the difference between your rating and the recruiters' on those items is a positive number, it means that you are not aware of the importance of those behaviors in establishing a long-term career plan for yourself. This represents a situation where you are expecting to find one thing when you start your career but actually may find something very different.

Finally, review all the value statements rated by the recruiters as either a 4 or 5 (i.e., not necessary for career success). Check to see if the difference between your ratings and theirs on those items are either zero or a positive number. (A difference of zero or a positive number would indicate that you also view the item as not very important for one's career success.) If the difference between your rating and the recruiters' on those items is a negative number, it means that you expect to engage in this behavior as part of your career strategy when, in reality, it may not help you at all.

WORK VALUES PROFILE

The following statements represent values that may be important to you in a work setting. For each item, rate the importance of the value to you at work. Use the rating scale to the right of the page.

1. **Ability Utilization:** I could do something that makes use of the full range of my abilities.
2. **Achievement:** The job gives me a feeling of personal accomplishment.
3. **Activity:** I could be busy all the time.
4. **Advancement:** The job provides an opportunity for advancement in the organization or profession.
5. **Authority:** I could formally tell people what to do.
6. **Autonomy:** I could make decisions on my own about what needs to be accomplished.
7. **Aesthetic:** I could be concerned with the form, beauty, and harmony of things around me.
8. **Affiliation:** I could have friendly interactions with others.
9. **Accrue Wealth:** I could accrue goods and wealth through my work.
10. **Clarity/Job Performance:** I could be clear about what I'm accomplishing on my job.
11. **Clarity/Organization:** I could be clear on how the organization is structured, its mission, goals, products, services, etc.
12. **Competition:** I could compete against others based on a clear standard of excellence.

* IMPORTANCE	RECRUITER AVERAGE		
1 Not Important 2-4 Average Importance 5 Extremely Important	MINUS (-)	RECRUITER'S IMPORTANCE	EQUAL
(CIRCLE ONE)			
1 2 3 4 5	-	4	= ______
1 2 3 4 5	-	4	= ______
1 2 3 4 5	-	2	= ______
1 2 3 4 5	-	4	= ______
1 2 3 4 5	-	2	= ______
1 2 3 4 5	-	4	= ______
1 2 3 4 5	-	2	= ______
1 2 3 4 5	-	3	= ______
1 2 3 4 5	-	3	= ______
1 2 3 4 5	-	4	= ______
1 2 3 4 5	-	4	= ______
1 2 3 4 5	-	3	= ______

13. **Compensation:** My pay and benefits would compare well with that of other workers.

14. **Compensation:** I could be properly rewarded for the work I do.

15. **Co-workers:** My co-workers would be easy to make friends with.

16. **Creativity:** I could uncover new ideas and more effective ways to do things.

17. **Development:** I could grow and develop my talents on the job.

18. **Economic:** I could do things that are useful and practical.

19. **Fairness:** The organization would administer its policies fairly.

20. **Fairness:** The organization would treat people without bias or prejudice.

21. **Happiness:** I could achieve a positive emotional state through my work.

22. **Honesty:** I could be honest and have integrity in my dealings with others.

23. **Independence:** I could work alone on the job.

24. **Influence:** I could achieve influence in the organization.

25. **Moral Values:** I could do the work without feeling that it is morally wrong.

IMPORTANCE	RECRUITER AVERAGE		
1 Not Important 2-4 Average Importance 5 Extremely Important	MINUS (-)	RECRUITER'S IMPORTANCE	EQUAL
(CIRCLE ONE)			
1 2 3 4 5	-	4	= ______
1 2 3 4 5	-	4	= ______
1 2 3 4 5	-	2	= ______
1 2 3 4 5	-	3	= ______
1 2 3 4 5	-	4	= ______
1 2 3 4 5	-	3	= ______
1 2 3 4 5	-	4	= ______
1 2 3 4 5	-	4	= ______
1 2 3 4 5	-	3	= ______
1 2 3 4 5	-	4	= ______
1 2 3 4 5	-	2	= ______
1 2 3 4 5	-	4	= ______
1 2 3 4 5	-	3	= ______

26. **Networking:** I could develop networks of people on my job.

27. **Participation:** I could give input on decisions that affect me.

28. **Power:** I could achieve influence over others directly.

29. **Productivity:** Conditions would allow me to be as productive as I could be.

30. **Recognition:** I could get recognition for the work I do.

31. **Security:** The job would provide for steady employment.

32. **Social Service:** I could do things for other people.

33. **Social Status:** I could be "somebody" in the community.

34. **Supervision--Human Relations:** My boss would be a pleasant person to work for.

35. **Supervision--Technical:** My boss would understand the technical aspects of my job.

36. **Supervision--Upward Influence:** My boss would have influence with his/her supervisor that helps me perform my job.

37. **Theoretical:** I could empirically and rationally seek out the answers to questions.

38. **Variety:** I could change my work routine as desired.

IMPORTANCE	RECRUITER AVERAGE		
1 Not Important **2-4 Average Importance** **5 Extremely Important**	**MINUS (-)**	**RECRUITER'S IMPORTANCE**	**EQUAL**
(CIRCLE ONE)			
1 2 3 4 5	-	3	= _______
1 2 3 4 5	-	2	= _______
1 2 3 4 5	-	4	= _______
1 2 3 4 5	-	3	= _______
1 2 3 4 5	-	3	= _______
1 2 3 4 5	-	2	= _______
1 2 3 4 5	-	2	= _______
1 2 3 4 5	-	3	= _______
1 2 3 4 5	-	2	= _______
1 2 3 4 5	-	3	= _______
1 2 3 4 5	-	3	= _______
1 2 3 4 5	-	2	= _______
1 2 3 4 5	-	3	= _______

39. **Working Conditions:** The job would have good working conditions.

40. **Work Hard:** I could work hard at what I do.

41. **Wisdom:** I could develop a broader understanding of myself and the world around me.

IMPORTANCE	RECRUITER AVERAGE		
1 Not Important **2-4 Average Importance** **5 Extremely Important**	**MINUS (-)**	**RECRUITER'S IMPORTANCE**	**EQUAL**
(CIRCLE ONE)			
1 2 3 4 5	-	3	= ______
1 2 3 4 5	-	3	= ______
1 2 3 4 5	-	3	= ______

BEHAVIORS FOR CAREER SUCCESS PROFILE

The following statements represent behaviors that may or may not be necessary for long-term career success in your chosen field. For each item, rate the extent to which you agree or disagree that the statement will be necessary for the career path that you plan to undertake.

1 = Strongly Agree
2 = Agree
3 = Neither Agree nor Disagree
4 = Disagree
5 = Strongly Disagree

1. Take refresher courses (not in a degree program) on my own time.

2. Have one- to three-year career plans developed.

3. Work 50 hours or more per week regularly.

4. Socialize with my boss during work hours.

5. Change my work habits to suit the environment in which I'm working.

6. Develop long-term career interests and goals.

7. Hold back on stating my opinion on a subject sometimes, even when I have a good idea.

8. Obtain a graduate degree in my field.

9. Discuss personal things with my colleagues at work.

10. Work at the highest performance levels, even during times when this is difficult due to lack of corporate resources.

11. Work on assignments where there is ambiguity about the final desired outcome.

12. Read technical journals from my field on a regular basis.

13. Spend break and/or lunch time with my co-workers.

AGREE-DISAGREE	RECRUITER AVERAGE			
1 = Strongly Agree 2 = Agree 3 = Neither Agree nor Disagree 4= Disagree 5 = Strongly Disagree	MINUS (-)	RECRUITER'S	EQUAL	
(CIRCLE ONE)				
1 2 3 4 5	-	3	=	______
1 2 3 4 5	-	2	=	______
1 2 3 4 5	-	3	=	______
1 2 3 4 5	-	3	=	______
1 2 3 4 5	-	3	=	______
1 2 3 4 5	-	2	=	______
1 2 3 4 5	-	3	=	______
1 2 3 4 5	-	3	=	______
1 2 3 4 5	-	4	=	______
1 2 3 4 5	-	2	=	______
1 2 3 4 5	-	3	=	______
1 2 3 4 5	-	2	=	______
1 2 3 4 5	-	3	=	______

14. Attend professional seminars in my field on a regular basis.

15. Design interesting work projects for myself.

16. Admit when I have no expertise in an area.

17. Become aware of the "politics" of my company and who the players are.

18. Identify one mentor after whom I can model my career.

19. Ask my work director or supervisor for new projects when things get slow.

20. Find out the career paths and backgrounds of the individuals up to three levels above me.

21. Bring work home or spend time at the office at night and on the weekend.

22. Be able to identify at least two jobs in my current company that I could expect to be in ten years from any given date.

23. Socialize with my boss and other persons at her/his level and above, after work hours.

24. Accept spending several years working before achieving any real status within the company.

25. Spend more time worrying about the politics of my organization since "who you know" will be most important to getting ahead.

AGREE-DISAGREE	RECRUITER AVERAGE			
1 = Strongly Agree 2 = Agree 3 = Neither Agree nor Disagree 4= Disagree 5 = Strongly Disagree (CIRCLE ONE)	MINUS (-)	RECRUITER'S	EQUAL	
1 2 3 4 5	-	2	=	_______
1 2 3 4 5	-	2	=	_______
1 2 3 4 5	-	2	=	_______
1 2 3 4 5	-	2	=	_______
1 2 3 4 5	-	2	=	_______
1 2 3 4 5	-	2	=	_______
1 2 3 4 5	-	2	=	_______
1 2 3 4 5	-	3	=	_______
1 2 3 4 5	-	2	=	_______
1 2 3 4 5	-	3	=	_______
1 2 3 4 5	-	3	=	_______
1 2 3 4 5	-	4	=	_______

Bibliography

Branch, S., " America's Most Powerful Black Executive," *Black Enterprise*, February, 1993, p. 78.

Granville, William Jr., Baltimore, Maryland: Career Communications Group Inc., *Just Say Yes*, 1989.

Pascale, R., "Fitting New Employees Into The Company Culture," *Fortune*, May 28, 1984, pp.28-40.

Additional Reading

Cannon, Thomas C., *Survival Routines For Professionals: Moving Towards Corporate Success*, Prentice Hall, Englewood Cliffs, NJ 1988.

Davis, G. and Watson, G., *Black Life in Corporate America: Swimming in the Mainstream*, Anchor Press/Doubleday, 1982.

Edwards, A. and Polite, C.K., *Children of the Dream: The Psychology of Black Success*, Doubleday, 1992.

McCoy, F., "America's Most Powerful Black Executives," *Black Enterprise*, February 1992, p. 78.

Osher, B. and Campbell, S., *The Blue Chip Graduate*, Peachtree Publisher, LTD, Atlanta, GA 1987.

Reynolds, R., "Making It On Your First Job," *Black Enterprise*, February 1992, pp 131-138.

Spivey, W., *Succeeding In Corporate America*, Vantage Press, New York, 1991.

Wade B., *Company Man*, Anchor Books, Doubleday, New York, 1991.

Wanous, J. P., *Organizational Entry*, Addison-Wesley Publishing Co., Reading MA, 1980.

Yates, M., *Knock 'Em Dead*, Bob Adams Inc. Publishers, Holbrook, MA, 1992.

"The authors have made a monumental contribution to the customers of corporate America: African-American students. I recommend this book as required reading for every African American prior to their first day in industry. I commit to having at least ten copies and will use them as the foundation for my mentoring efforts."

Andrew L. Crowe
Director, Construction &
Minority Business Development
Eli Lilly and Company

"This is important reading for any African American seeking job opportunities, but also for anyone interested in corporate America as a career."

Ben Pope
Director of Human Resources
University of California Berkeley

"... an excellent beacon for students to follow. Students who read and assimilate the tips in this guide will have a competitive advantage over other students who are seeking the same position."

George R. Brewster
Program Manager, Human Resources
Corning Incorporated

"I wish I would have had access to the information shared in the manuscript when I graduated from college sixteen years ago. The book will also be a 'must read' for employers as well!"

Michael C. Hyter
Vice President of Public Affairs & Communications
Dayton's • Marshall Field's • Hudson's

"After 25 years it is easy to forget the Basics--and succeeding or surviving in the Corporate world is closely aligned to the basics--hard work, teamwork, risk taking, and having fun. *The Game* was an excellent reminder that great teams produce the largest numbers of great players (not vice versa) and that the basics when combined with positive energy and continuous improvement are key. My 12- and 13 year-old daughters, Candy and Cassie, will be required to read your book."

Mannie L. Jackson
Sr. Vice President, Corporate Marketing and Administration
Honeywell, Inc.

"I fully endorse the concepts you have introduced and believe it will have great impact on African-American students abilities to succeed in major companies."

Kennan W. Smith
Manager
Exxon Research and Engineering Company

"*The Game Called Industry: A Practical Career Guide for African-American Students* is filled with practical and timeless advice to the new professional in any industry. The profiles and values tests make it required reading before starting a new job."

Rosita Jackson
Associate Director
Career Services Office
Georgia Institute of Technology

"As a fellow corporate executive, I also have interviewed hundreds and hundreds of applicants. I just wish I could have had this publication when I was in college."

"This is well done, a must read for anyone that wants to be successful in this corporate world."

Michael Townsend
Logistics Services Manager
Digital Equipment Corporation

"I found this book to be very informative and well researched. It will enlighten African-American students and professionals about the mindset prevalent in today's work place. The book provides an accurate reflection of the corporate environment and reveals widely held misconceptions about corporate America. I believe the book will empower the reader to deal competitively in the market place. I can envision this book earning a place on many bookshelves, particularly those of corporate executives and universities. The book presents a challenge and a new perspective for the work place."

Leo P. Sam, Jr.
Vice President, University Relations/Public Affairs
Florida Agricultural and Mechanical University

"an excellent treatise on ways to enhance one's potential for success in industry. While this guide addresses a wide array of issues, it is simultaneously focused and practical. All aspirants for a career in industry can benefit significantly from this informative and insightful guide."

Mark Kiel
Chairman
North Carolina Agricultural and Technical State University

"As an experienced player in *The Game Called Industry*, I found the authors' advice right on the mark. This book will help all students, African-American or otherwise, understand the formal <u>and</u> informal rules that companies play by to hire and promote all employees."

"My only criticism of the book is that it wasn't available 15 years ago when I could have really used it."

Joseph M. George
Business Unit Director, Schools/Colleges
Honeywell

"You have provided the reader ... with some valuable work tactics and strategies which can only help those minority graduates who will be entering the workplace in the near future. This book could be one of the premier or the best role model for those minorities entering the world of work."

Shedrick E. Williams Jr.
Collins & Aikman

"*The Game Called Industry* charts a course for African-American students preparing to enter the work world. This course begins first with self-knowledge. What are my values and expectations? In what way can I contribute to the organization goals? How can the organization help me meet my own personal goals and development plan? Next, an assessment of the organization is necessary. What are the values and goals of the organization? Who succeeds and what are the requirements for success? Are these values and goals consistent with my own goals? Only when the last question is answered in the affirmative can a relationship that is based on trust be established. While African-American students are learning this key lesson about adaptation and flexibility, it is also important that they know that the world's great organizations are taking steps to become more flexible and responsive to the needs of today's workforce."

Carolyn Irving
Workforce Diversity Manager
Medtronic, Inc.

"It is a thought provoking text, recognizing the historical perspective of African Americans in industry and issuing a blueprint for the upcoming graduate and new employee of the corporate workforce. In your manuscript, you have succinctly given both the graduate and the new employee an opportunity to examine her/his perspectives of industry. The reader can then compare that perspective with the perspectives and hindsight of the professionals who are the most experienced with the day-to-day environs of many corporations. In my experience of over twenty-three years of working with the careers of younger professionals, this text is one of the few that particularly addresses our African-American students."

Ann Davis Shaw
Associate Director of Career Services and Preprofessional Advising
Massachusetts Institute of Technology

"I do believe that the book is a much needed reference for minority college graduates. It provides answers to questions and highlights things that students need to know."

Harold L. Martin, Ph.D., PE
Dean of Engineering
North Carolina Agricultural and Technical State University

"After reading *The Game Called Industry: A Practical Career Guide for African-American Students*, students will have a solid basis for analyzing and selecting options to make a successful transition from college to a rewarding career."

"The Guide is clearly written and easy to understand. It translates the authors' many years of experience into an excellent implementation guide for creating a clear path to a successful career."

Cleotha Jackson
Director, Corporate Human Resources and Workforce Diversity
Blue Cross Blue Shield of Massachusetts

"The document is simple and basic, which makes for easy reading and learning. Technically, the document is accurate."

Curtis L. White
Vice President, Corporate Diversity
Honeywell, Inc.

"Overall, I think this book is impressive for these reasons:

(1) Choosing an employer will never be a scientific process, but by providing tools for candidates to assess the degree to which their values align with a company's values is useful to both.

(2) You emphasize not only that career development is largely a self-development process, but also the significant personal commitment which must be made today to advance in the corporate world.

(3) The information contained, while directed to African Americans, has applicability for everyone regardless of race or gender."

Henry S. Halaiko
Outreach Strategy Consultant
Mobil Corporation

"... a thorough review of the necessary attributes African-American students need to process in order to embark on successful business careers. Lawrence and Sheppeck have provided a practical guide to students just out of college, as well as those who have been seeking to better understand the barriers and opportunities that must be addressed for upward movement in the business world. I recommend this as required reading for students, college professors, and the leaders of America's businesses."

Dr. Richard Green
President
Metropolitan State University

"*The Game Called Industry* is an insightful look into the issues facing young African-American transitioning into the corporate world. Reading this book should be required reading for all African-American college students, placement offices, and corporate recruiters. I wish this had existed when I graduate from college."

Myron L. Hardiman
Department Head
Eli Lilly and Company

There will always be a natural tension between the way things are and the way we believe things should be. Recognizing this early on is important if we are to have any real chance to create better opportunities for ourselves. *The Game Called Industry* is a good first step toward bringing that realization into focus.

Kenneth R. Garrett
Director, Human Resources
FMC Corporation

"This is an excellent and useful tool for college students transitioning into Corporate America. It provides good information on how to prepare for a successful entry into Corporate America which will lead to a successful career. This is also very valuable for industry recruiters which will provide meaningful insight on minority recruiting and retention."

Gerald E. Wiley
Director, Human Resources
Monsanto

"It is often said it is up to us to give something back. In the book *The Game Called Industry: A Practical Career Guide for African-American Students*, Tom Lawrence has gone well beyond the expectation that 'each one, teach one'. He has taught many through his 25 years of industry experience. This book will help teach many more in the future. I strongly recommend it to all students beginning their job/career search process."

William A. Dittmore
Director of Recruitment and College Relations
General Mills, Inc.

"Shadowing you, Tom, while recruiting has taught me a number of valuable ($) lessons, some of which are:

* Identify the learners who will be outstanding professionals.

* Know the professionals who have a strong interest in learners. (Notice the names you've mentioned in *The Game*...)"

Willis F. Baker
President
Willis F. Baker & Associates

"I found the book to be extremely informative. As a new manager in the College Recruiting arena, it was enlightening to me to find so many examples that I can use in my college recruitment, retention, and development programs."

"For college students, this book will be an eye opener for a lot of them. Because they have finished school, or about to finish school, and have a good GPA, they are working on the assumption that they will get exciting positions with their eyes closed because they are AFRICAN AMERICAN and superstars. NOT SO. The section on politics is crucial. I could go on and on because I enjoyed it so much (selfishly soaking in all the new ideas)."

Florence Jones
Manager, University Relations
Polaroid

"This book provides practical, direct, realistic advice and to African-American students on effective ways to evaluate and understand their new environment in corporate America. Learning the unspoken norms of a corporation is critical to the success of any employee, and this book provides easy to follow guidelines on how to identify these norms. Further, it offers guidelines to help students successfully integrate into their new environment and develop good working relationships with their manager and peers. Any student who reads *The Game Called Industry* and follows the practical tips offered is sure to be successful as he or he enters the world of corporate America."

"As a manager, I, too, found this book to be very useful. It provided me with insight into understanding certain behaviors of some students who were new to the workforce and lacked a parent role model to provide them with information on the unspoken norms of working in corporate America. It is certainly a useful tool to have as managers begin to increasingly manage more diverse workgroups."

Yvonne L. Craycroft
Manager, Diversity Programs
Apple Computer, Inc.

"Significant reading for the young minority man or woman on 'The Real Deal' about succeeding in the corporate tangle!"

"It is a big help to address what is not taught in the classroom."

Harold T. Epps
General Manager
Inner City, Inc.

"Practical, on target, useful. These are the terms that come to mind when I read Tom Lawrence's book entitled *The Game Called Industry: A Practical Career Guide for African-American Students*."

"Lawrence's comments begin by setting a framework both historically and from a contemporary viewpoint. It should be 'must' reading for all young African Americans who feel that they want to work in industry. The book provides real insight into the corporate culture, which it is imperative to know and understand if you are to achieve any success in that environment. The bottom line is you cannot know too much about the environment in which you work. The quantitative portion of the book adds a dimension seldom available in one publication. Dr. Sheppeck's surveys can help you identify those specific areas in which African-American students would be well advised to gain more information. Tom Lawrence's insightful and practical advice merges well with the empirical data provided by the skillful assessment of Dr. Sheppeck's work. Their cogent message should give any budding young industrialist a distinct advantage on his or her way to the top."

Samuel M. Hall, Jr.
Director Career Services Office
Howard University

"*The Game Called Industry*: The book is a long overdue bridge for minority students entering the "real world" upon graduation. What has been a piecemeal approach in the past is now a condensed package that gives students a real chance of understanding the challenge of who they really are and the impact that they can have on the organization and the organization can have on them. A job well done."

Vernon Martin
Manager of Training and Human Resources Development
Olin Corporation

"I have thoroughly enjoyed over 25 years of professional and personal friendship with you and no one is better qualified to document the experience of Corporate America and a suggested success formula. As the majority owner of the Harlem Globetrotters, I am in constant contact with the public, with educators, and the men and women who comprise this great organization."

"Throughout the years, the Harlem Globetrotters have created magical fun and mystique for people of all ages, all shapes, and all sizes. This magic has been performed in over 100 countries and has been seen by hundreds of millions of fans. In 1951, the Globetrotters set a basketball attendance record that still stands today (75,000 fans packed the Olympic Stadium in Berlin, West Germany). A civil war was suspended for four days to allow the Globetrotters to play a few games in Peru. When the team departed, the war resumed. The Globetrotters have performed in front of three Popes."

"The typical career of a professional athlete is three to five years. Following that joyful period, the business of life begins and 'The Game' of surviving and scoring points in the work world becomes their new mission. I liked your message and was impressed with the skill at which you captured both the subtle and not-so-subtle nuances of the Corporate world...my hope is that every player on our team, during their travels around the globe, will read and learn from your book. To you, Tom Lawrence, we thank you for taking the time to contribute to the future of others."

Mannie L. Jackson
Chairman and CEO
Harlem Globetrotters

"The book covers real topics of vital interest to African-American youth of today."

John Foster, Ph.D., P.E.
Dean, College of Engineering and Architecture
Prairie View A&M University

"*The Game Called Industry: A Practical Career Guide for African-American Students* should be a bestseller among students. This book is certainly a much needed tool for anyone making the transition from college to industry. As we continue to deal with retention in the workforce, especially among African-American employees, this book will provide the guidance that is needed to help them succeed."

Della Smith
Manager Strategic Programs
Intel Corporation

"The authors have contributed in supplying much needed guidance for young people who wish to enter into employment in corporate America. The authors have shown an understanding of the desires and needs of the emerging generation of students. Your knowledge and comments about corporate America based on your years of experience working within Honeywell's higher echelon combined with your knowledge of the Afro-American community suggest that this manuscript should be required reading for all corporate executives."

Kenneth I. Guscott
General Partner
Long Bay Management Company

"Simply outstanding! As I read the manuscript, I found myself agreeing and felt reassured that information shared with technical students is on target. It is my belief that until students understand the 'Game,' and develop a master game plan (strategy) for success, they will continue to be frustrated by corporate America."

R. Guy Vickers
Executive Director
Southeastern Consortium for Minorities in Engineering

How I Got My Dream Job

And How You Can Get Yours, Too

by Scott V. Edwards

Scott V. Edwards found himself in the worst job market since the Great Depression, but he was determined to get a job before graduation. And he did. In fact, he got the job that met his career objective, his dream job. Now, he shares his successful job search strategies with college students. Scott graduated in May 1993 from Howard University with a BBA degree in finance.

Price: $6.95 (including shipping and handling)
See order form or send $6.95 to:

How I Got My Dream Job
THE BLACK COLLEGIAN
1240 So. Broad St.
New Orleans, LA 70125

JOB OPPORTUNITIES '94

A Guide to Employment Opportunities for African-American Students

JOB OPPORTUNITIES '94 is the single most comprehensive listing of equal opportunity employers. Over 175 employers are listed with contact information, majors recruited, and how to apply. *JOB OPPORTUNITIES '94* also includes feature articles on the job search process and job-hunting strategies.

Price: $12.00 (including shipping and handling)
See order form or send $12.00 to:

JOB OPPORTUNITIES '94
THE BLACK COLLEGIAN Magazine
1240 So. Broad St.
New Orleans, LA 70125

ORDER FORM

☐ Subscription to ***The Black Collegian***

	☐ 1 year	$12.00
	☐ 2 years	$20.00

☐ ***JOB OPPORTUNITIES '94*** $12.00

☐ ***Guide To Graduate and Professional Fellowships*** $12.00

☐ ***How I Got My Dream Job*** $6.95

☐ ***The Game Called Industry*** $6.95

Total Enclosed $ ___________

Name ______________________________________
Address ____________________________________
City _________________ State ______ Zip ________

Please mail this form to:

Books
THE BLACK COLLEGIAN
1240 South Broad Street
New Orleans, LA 70125

THE JOB FINDER, a free service of THE BLACK COLLEGIAN, is a high-tech job search program that matches job candidates with leading national employers who are seeking to fill vacant positions. When you register with THE JOB FINDER, your credentials immediately go on line to hundreds of hiring managers at major corporations and government agencies across the country.

To join THE JOB FINDER Database, send a self-addressed, stamped envelope to THE BLACK COLLEGIAN, 1240 So. Broad St., New Orleans, LA 70125. We will send you THE JOB FINDER Candidate Registration Form.